MORE VISUALIZATION SKILLS FOR READING COMPREHENSION

SIX-MINUTE THINKING SKILLS

WORKBOOK

HAPPY FROG PRESS

Print ISBN 978-1-989505-18-2

Ebook ISBN 978-1-989505-19-9

Happy Frog Press

www.HappyFrogPress.com

INTRODUCTION

Welcome to **More Visualization Skills for Reading Comprehension**. This workbook builds on our best-selling 'Visualization Skills' workbook to provide more scaffolded practice for learners still building their comprehension skills.

The first quarter of this workbook mimics the step-by-step activities found in the original workbook, building visualization skills from single words to 2-sentence paragraphs. Those who have completed the first workbook can use these early pages as a review. If this section moves too fast for your learner, the original 'Visualization Skills' workbook may be a more successful choice.

The remainder of the book builds skill from 2-sentence paragraphs to short multi-paragraph texts. This positions your learner for a successful transition to real books.

WHY IS VISUALIZATION IMPORTANT?

Visualization is our ability to create mental pictures in our heads based on the text we read or the words we hear. It is one of the key skills required for reading comprehension.

Students who visualize as they read not only have a richer reading experience but can recall what they have read for longer periods of time.

Moreover, having a strong mental image of a text allows students to more accurately and effectively answer Higher Order Thinking (HOT) questions, such as inferencing, prediction, etc.

If your learner struggles with reading comprehension, working on visualization skills should be high on your list of priorities.

ABOUT THIS WORKBOOK

Key details of this workbook are:

- Suitable for 1-1 or classroom use

  This book can be used in a classroom or with a single learner.

- Gradually increments difficulty

  Learners begin with simple visualization tasks, which gradually increment as the book progresses. By the end, learners visualize multi-paragraph fiction and non-fiction passages.

- No-prep. No extra materials required

Everything needed is included in the book - except for a pencil or pen! The student can write their answers in the book, or use a piece of paper if the book needs to be reused.

- Small chunks. Use any time

  Our worksheets are designed for 'six-minute sessions.' Anytime you have a spare moment, your learner can accomplish the next incremental step in their learning journey.

The ability to visualize as you read is key for school and learning success. Support your struggling readers with this fun, engaging workbook that will build your learner's ability and confidence in this important skill.

HOW TO COACH A SIX-MINUTE SESSION

No student wants to spend extra time learning. Follow the guidelines in this section to promote efficient and motivating progress for your student.

1. Have a consistent and regular schedule.

Consistency and regularity are important if you want to reach a goal. So, choose a regular schedule for your six-minute sessions, get your learner's agreement and stick to it!

In a school setting, make this task a regular part of your students' day. In a home setting, aim for 3-4 times per week.

2. Devise a reward system.

Working on skill deficits is hard work for any learner. Appreciate your student's effort by building in a reward system.

This may include a reward when a specific number of exercises are finished, when tasks are completed correctly on the first try, or whatever specific goal will encourage your learner at this point in their journey.

Remember to reward based on effort as well as correctness.

3. Include time for review and correction.

After your student has completed the activity, review your student's work.

When identifying an error, make a positive statement and then provide the least information needed for the learner to make a correction. For example, prefer:

> *Nice job. I can see you have drawn the desk and the pen. There is one more thing mentioned in the text. Can you see it and draw it?*

to:

> *You forgot to draw the chair.*

The first method develops the student's ability to review their work and find the error. This valuable skill will lead to fewer errors in future worksheets.

The second method simply tells the student what to do.

Another good technique for reviewing is to ask your learner open questions. (Not Yes/No questions). If you see your learner create an image that does not fit the text, help them question their images. Ask questions like, "What does the text say about what the boy was doing?", "What did the text say about WHERE this was happening?"

Make sure that your learner always has a chance to physically correct their work.

4. Don't evaluate drawing skills

During the workbook, your learner sketches what he or she has pictured for a text. This drawing is a representation of the mental image that your learner has created.

The quality of the drawing is completely irrelevant. A simple sketch is all that is needed. The only requirement is that you can recognize — or your learner can explain — how the drawing matches the text.

Don't let your learner spend time elaborating the drawing or making it 'perfect'. A quick representation is all that is needed. It is the mental work to create the image that we want to build, not the manual proficiency to transfer it to the page.

For this reason we have quite small spaces available for the drawings in the workbook - to promote quick sketches instead of elaborate drawings. If your learner has fine motor issues and needs a bigger space, just grab some paper instead.

5. Do the whole book twice!

The first time you go through the workbook, follow the directions as written. This will help your learner build basic visualization skills.

When you reach the end, start back at the beginning, this time completing the exercises orally. This extra practice will develop your learner's visualization skills even further.

The second time through, instead of drawing their mental

image, your learner will describe to you the images they are creating.

This is harder work for your learner, but is excellent practice for building visualization skills.

Make sure to use questioning to elicit further details from your learner.

6. Ask questions to get more details

A really important part of helping your learner develop visualization skills is to ask questions to help your learner develop a richer picture.

Use the nine visualization words below (taught in the workbook) to ask your learner for more details about their mental image.

WHAT, WHERE, WHEN, ACTION, EMOTION, RELATION, HOW, VISUAL DETAILS, OTHER SENSORY DETAILS

For example:

- Where is your picture happening?
- I can see you've drawn a house. What is it made of?
- Are there any smells?
- Is the train in front of the tree?

Two types of questions are recommended:

1. Open questions that use a WH word. These are words like WHO, WHAT, WHERE, etc. Answers to these questions are more detailed than answers to simple Yes/No questions.

2. Alternative options questions. These questions are best for learners who struggle with expressive language, or who are still getting used to describing their images. These are questions like:

- Is the train big or small?
- I am trying to picture the house you mentioned, is it one level or two?

Be careful of getting too detailed with your questions. Ask about the most important elements and don't spend time questioning for the exact size and color of a tiny flower in the background!

Think of your job as questioning for the types of elements that might be included in a summary.

To help you formulate your questions, samples for each question word can be found in the next chapter.

7. Most importantly....

Most importantly, make this a FUN experience with your learner!

Learning happens best when our brains are relaxed, not stressed. It is your job to make sure your student's brain stays ready to learn while doing this workbook. Build success upon success and celebrate every small achievement.

COACHING QUESTIONS

Use the question words and these sample questions as a starting point for your own questions.

WHAT

What things are in your picture?

What's the most noticeable thing in your picture?

WHERE

Where is the boy in your picture?

What is around the boy in your picture?

WHEN

When is your picture happening?

Is it day or night time in your picture? How can you tell?

ACTION

What actions are people doing in your picture?

What movement is happening in your picture?

EMOTION

How are people feeling in your picture?

What are people's faces showing in your picture?

RELATION

What's at the front of your picture?

The train you mentioned, is that in front of the tree or behind the tree?

HOW

You said your boy was sitting. Is he sitting up straight or slouching down?

You mentioned a stream. How is the water flowing? Is it fast and deep, or shallow and slow?

VISUAL DETAILS

Tell me what the girl looks like. How old is she? What is she wearing?

How big is that tree?

OTHER SENSORY DETAILS

Are there any smells in your picture?

What sounds can the people in your picture hear?

IMAGE WORDS - WHEN

Circle the words that mention WHEN something happens.

Draw something that conveys the WHEN of the sentence.

Kevin walked to school at 7 am.

Gina was very excited that today was Christmas Day.

Coaching Note: WHEN can be difficult to draw. Be generous in your interpretation.

IMAGE WORDS - WHAT + WHEN + WHERE

Draw the sentence showing WHAT, WHEN and WHERE.

Alex practiced shooting baskets in the back yard last night.

Lisa went ice skating on the pond near her house.

Coaching Note: The WHEN in the second example is a season rather than a time.

IMAGE WORDS - HOW

Some words tell us HOW things happen - fast, slow, sadly, etc.

Underline any words that describe HOW.

Draw a picture to match the sentence.

Hallie carefully hammered the nail into the wall.

Kevin threw on his clothes and dashed out the door.

IMAGE WORDS - VISUAL DETAILS

Some words tell us what things look like. These are VISUAL DETAILS.

Underline any words that describe a VISUAL DETAIL.

Draw a picture to match the sentence.

The present was wrapped in red sparkly paper and tied with a huge green bow.

The tiny kitten was white with cute grey ears.

IMAGE WORDS - OTHER SENSORY DETAILS

Good writers use all five senses to convey information. Look in the following sentences for OTHER SENSORY DETAILS such as touch, taste, sound and smell.

Underline any words that describe an OTHER SENSORY DETAIL.

Draw a picture to match the text.

The trees rustled with the light breeze.

The smell of warm, freshly baked bread drifted from the kitchen.

Draw the sentence showing HOW, VISUAL DETAILS and
OTHER SENSORY DETAILS.

**Jim stared in admiration at Cassie's new hair style.
It was short, spiky and bright blue.**

**The bees buzzed lazily from flower to flower in the
hot summer sun.**

VISUAL RECALL: PART 1

Look at the picture below for up to 30 seconds. Try to visualize the picture in your mind.

'Visualize' means using your imagination to make the picture in your mind. For some people, closing their eyes makes it easier to visualize.

When you can visualize the picture, turn the page and follow the instructions.

VISUAL RECALL: PART 2

Visualize the picture from the previous page in your head. Note down all the details you can remember in the table. No going back to check!

Some details may not be shown in the picture.

WHAT	
WHERE	
WHEN	
ACTION	
EMOTION	
RELATION	
SENSORY DETAILS (see, touch, taste, sound, smell)	

How many details did you visualize?_____

Write a one sentence summary of the picture.

SPATIAL MANIPULATION

Look at the picture below.

Visualize this image in your mind. Replace the horizontal lines with a picture of a tree. Now turn the whole picture upside down.

Draw the new picture in the space below.

LETTER SEQUENCE

Look at the letter sequence below and visualize it in your mind.

Cover up the letters and answer the questions. Don't peek!

GBTY

1. What is the second letter?
2. What is the last letter?
3. List the letters in reverse order.

Answer the same questions for the following sequence.

Don't peek!

NLSWR

VISUAL DIRECTIONS - INSTRUCTIONS

Read the drawing directions below and visualize what you need to draw.

Reread the directions if you need to. When you have a good picture in your mind of what you need to draw, turn the page and draw the picture.

Once you have turned the page, don't look back. Just do your best.

DRAWING INSTRUCTIONS

1. Draw a large square.
2. In the middle of the square, draw two small triangles, one above the other.
3. Color the top triangle black.
4. Draw a small circle below the square.

VISUAL DIRECTIONS - DRAWING

Keep the image in your mind and draw the picture below.

ITEM MEMORY PART 1

Look at the pictures below and visualize them in your mind.

After 30 seconds, turn the page and list or draw everything that you can remember.

Don't peek!

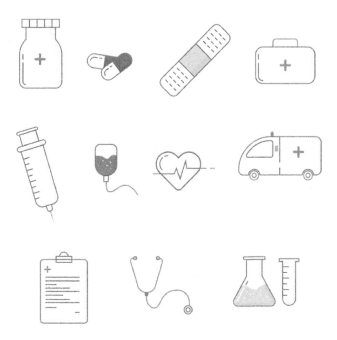

ITEM MEMORY PART 2

List or draw every item that you can remember.

Don't peek!

56. MOTION FROM TEXT: INSTRUCTIONS

Read the text once or twice. Visualize the scene as you read, making sure to include the characters' movement in your 'brain movie.'

Cover the text. Now stand up and act out the story in the text. Include as many details as you can remember.

Turn the page and complete the tasks. Don't look back! (Only do one text at a time.)

TEXT 1

Kerry stood up to bat. She missed the first ball and the umpire called 'strike'. After a deep slow breath, she got ready for the second ball and swung for it. Crack! She hit it. A home run!

Act out this story now.

TEXT 2

Jack finished his dinner and took his plate to the sink. He didn't feel like doing homework, but he had a math test tomorrow. He picked up his books and went to his room to study.

Act out this story now.

Coaching Note: Use questioning to help your learner include as many details from the text as possible into their movements.

TEXT 1

On the left, draw how Kerry might feel after the first ball.

On the right, draw how Kerry might feel after the second ball.

TEXT 2

Draw what Jack did first. Then draw what Jack did next.

TWO SENTENCES TO IMAGE: INSTRUCTIONS

Read the text below. Visualize the story as you read. Include as many details as you can.

Next, turn the page and draw an image from the movie you created in your brain. Include as many details as you can. Don't look back!

Do one text at a time.

TEXT 1

It was pouring rain and Henry did not want to walk to school. He sighed as he put on his rain coat.

Turn the page now.

TEXT 2

Ken bounced in his seat as he waited for the school bell to ring. His grandparents were coming to visit today and he couldn't wait to see them.

Turn the page now.

TWO SENTENCES TO IMAGE: DRAWING

TEXT 1: Draw a picture from your brain movie.

TEXT 2: Draw a picture from your brain movie.

Coaching Note: Use questions to elicit more details about your learner's image.

TWO SENTENCES TO TABLE 1: PART 1

Read the text below. Visualize the story as you read. Include as many details as you can in your brain movie.

Next, turn the page and list all the details you remember from your brain movie. Don't look back!

Katie couldn't believe her luck. Today was the sports carnival at school and she was sick.

Coaching Note: Explain any words that your learner does not understand. You can't make an image if you don't know what to visualize!

TWO SENTENCES TO TABLE 1: PART 2

Note down all the details you can remember from your brain movie or from the story in the table below. No going back to check!

Some sections of the table may not have any details.

WHAT	
WHERE	
WHEN	
ACTION	
EMOTION	
RELATION	
SENSORY DETAILS (see, touch, taste, sound, smell)	

How many details did you visualize?_____

Write a short one sentence summary of the story.

TWO SENTENCES TO QUESTIONS: PART 1

Read the text below. Visualize the story as you read. Include as many details as you can in your brain movie.

Next, turn the page and answer the questions about the brain movie you created. Don't look back!

Diabetes is a disease that occurs when your blood glucose levels are too high. Blood glucose is your main source of energy and comes from the food you eat.

Coaching Note: Explain any words that your learner does not understand. You can't make an image if you don't know what to visualize!

TWO SENTENCES TO QUESTIONS: PART 2

Visualize the story from the previous page in your head and answer these questions.

What disease was mentioned?

Do you imagine diabetes being a good thing or a bad thing?

What words made you imagine diabetes was a good/bad thing?

What did you imagine for "the food you eat"?

PARAGRAPH TO IMAGE: PART 1

Read the text below. Visualize the story as you read. Include as many details as you can.

Next, turn the page and draw an image from the movie you created in your brain. Include as many details as you can. Don't look back!

Do one text at a time.

TEXT 1

Penguins lay their eggs on land. Mostly, the birds all nest together in a large group. This group is called a rookery. The father and mother take turns keeping the egg warm. When they are not on the nest, they swim in the ocean looking for food.

Turn the page now.

TEXT 2

The Appalachians are the longest group of mountains in eastern North America. These mountains start in the northern U.S. state of Maine. They end in the southern state of Georgia. The Appalachian Trail through the mountains is about 2,200 miles long.

Turn the page now.

TEXT 1: Draw a picture from your brain movie.

TEXT 2: Draw a picture from your brain movie.

Coaching Note: Use questions to elicit more details about your learner's image.

PARAGRAPH TO IMAGE: PART 1

Read the text below. Visualize the story as you read. Include as many details as you can.

Do one text at a time.

TEXT 1

The Oregon Trail is a 2,170-mile historic wagon route in the United States that connected the Missouri River to valleys in Oregon. The trail passed through what is now Kansas, Nebraska, Wyoming, Idaho and Oregon.

Turn the page now.

TEXT 2

An allergy occurs when the body's immune system sees a substance as harmful and overreacts to it. The substances that cause allergic reactions are allergens. Allergies are one of the most common chronic diseases.

Turn the page now.

Coaching Note: Explain any words that your learner does not understand. You can't make an image if you don't know what to visualize!

PARAGRAPH TO IMAGE: PART 2

TEXT 1: Draw a picture from your brain movie.

TEXT 2: Draw a picture from your brain movie.

Coaching Note: Use questions to elicit more details about your learner's image.

PARAGRAPH TO IMAGE: PART 1

Read the text below. Visualize the story as you read. Include as many details as you can.

Next, turn the page and draw an image from the movie you created in your brain. Include as many details as you can. Don't look back!

Do one text at a time.

TEXT 1

Worms are very interesting creatures. They do not have lungs or other breathing organs. Instead they breathe through their skin. Their skin also produces a fluid that makes moving through underground burrows easier.

Turn the page now.

TEXT 2

What is space junk? Space junk is any piece of machinery or rubbish left by humans in space. Space junk may be big, like a dead satellite. Or it can be tiny, like small paint flecks.

Turn the page now.

PARAGRAPH TO IMAGE: PART 2

TEXT 1: Draw a picture from your brain movie.

TEXT 2: Draw a picture from your brain movie.

Coaching Note: Use questions to elicit more details about your learner's image.

PARAGRAPH TO IMAGE: PART 1

Read the text below. Visualize the story as you read. Include as many details as you can.

Do one text at a time.

TEXT 1

The world's tallest sandcastle was nearly 58 feet high. It was built in Germany in 2019 for a competition. An international team of 12 sculptors and eight technicians from Russia, Poland, Hungary, Germany, Holland and Latvia created the huge structure in three-and-a-half weeks.

Turn the page now.

TEXT 2

Mercury is the smallest planet in our solar system and the closest to the sun. The planet orbits the sun in only 88 Earth days, faster than any other planet in our solar system.

Turn the page now.

TEXT 1: Draw a picture from your brain movie.

TEXT 2: Draw a picture from your brain movie.

Coaching Note: Use questions to elicit more details about your learner's image.

PARAGRAPH TO TABLE: PART 1

Read the text below. Visualize the story as you read. Include as many details as you can in your brain movie.

Next, turn the page and list all the details you remember from your brain movie. Don't look back!

Everything around us is made of matter—your hair, plants, even the air you breathe! There are four states of matter: liquid, gas, solid, and plasma. Water is an example of a liquid. Steam is an example of a gas. Ice is an example of a solid. The sun is an example of plasma.

Coaching Note: Explain any words that your learner does not understand. You can't make an image if you don't know what to visualize!

PARAGRAPH TO TABLE: PART 2

Note down all the details you can remember from your brain movie or from the story in the table below. No going back to check!

Some sections of the table may not have any details.

WHAT	
WHERE	
WHEN	
ACTION	
EMOTION	
RELATION	
SENSORY DETAILS (see, touch, taste, sound, smell)	

How many details did you visualize?_____

Write a one or two sentence summary of the text.

_____

_____

PARAGRAPH TO TABLE: PART 1

Read the text below. Visualize the story as you read. Include as many details as you can in your brain movie.

Next, turn the page and list all the details you remember from your brain movie. Don't look back!

The Hoover Dam is a concrete dam that blocks the Colorado River on the border between Nevada and Arizona in the U.S. It was finished in 1936 and was the largest dam in the world at that time. The lake behind it is called Lake Mead. The dam and Lake Mead are popular tourist destinations.

Coaching Note: Explain any words that your learner does not understand. You can't make an image if you don't know what to visualize!

PARAGRAPH TO TABLE: PART 2

Note down all the details you can remember from your brain movie or from the story in the table below. No going back to check!

Some sections of the table may not have any details.

WHAT	
WHERE	
WHEN	
ACTION	
EMOTION	
RELATION	
SENSORY DETAILS (see, touch, taste, sound, smell)	

How many details did you visualize?_____

Write a one or two sentence summary of the story.

PARAGRAPH TO TABLE: PART 1

Read the text below. Visualize the story as you read. Include as many details as you can in your brain movie.

Next, turn the page and list all the details you remember from your brain movie. Don't look back!

Carlsbad Caverns National Park is a national park in New Mexico. Carlsbad Caverns is one of the oldest and most famous cave systems in the world. The caverns include several vast underground chambers, up to 250 feet high, filled with amazing formations of many colors and shapes.

Coaching Note: Explain any words that your learner does not understand. You can't make an image if you don't know what to visualize!

PARAGRAPH TO TABLE: PART 2

Note down all the details you can remember from your brain movie or from the story in the table below. No going back to check!

Some sections of the table may not have any details.

WHAT	
WHERE	
WHEN	
ACTION	
EMOTION	
RELATION	
SENSORY DETAILS (see, touch, taste, sound, smell)	

How many details did you visualize?_____

Write a one or two sentence summary of the story.

PARAGRAPH TO TABLE: PART 1

Read the text below. Visualize the story as you read. Include as many details as you can in your brain movie.

Next, turn the page and list all the details you remember from your brain movie. Don't look back!

Singapore is an island country in Southeast Asia. It is quite near the equator. The country is home to 5.7 million people. There are four official languages: English, Malay, Chinese and Tamil. Singapore's culture, food and festivals are very diverse because of its rich cultural history.

Coaching Note: Explain any words that your learner does not understand. You can't make an image if you don't know what to visualize!

PARAGRAPH TO TABLE: PART 2

Note down all the details you can remember from your brain movie or from the story in the table below. No going back to check!

Some sections of the table may not have any details.

WHAT	
WHERE	
WHEN	
ACTION	
EMOTION	
RELATION	
SENSORY DETAILS (see, touch, taste, sound, smell)	

How many details did you visualize?_____

Write a one or two sentence summary of the story.

PARAGRAPH TO QUESTIONS: PART 1

Read the text below. Visualize the story as you read. Include as many details as you can in your brain movie.

Next, turn the page and answer the questions about the brain movie you created. Don't look back!

The piano is a musical instrument invented in Italy around the year 1700. It is played using a keyboard of back and white keys. The piano was different from previous, similar instruments because it could be played loudly or softly.

Coaching Note: Explain any words that your learner does not understand. You can't make an image if you don't know what to visualize!

PARAGRAPH TO QUESTIONS: PART 2

Visualize the previous text and answer these questions.

Describe the piano in your movie.

_____

_____

Where was the piano invented?

_____

_____

The piano was invented in 1700. What things did you visualize in your brain movie to show 1700?

_____

_____

PARAGRAPH TO QUESTIONS: PART 1

Read the text below. Visualize the story as you read. Include as many details as you can in your brain movie.

Next, turn the page and answer the questions about the brain movie you created. Don't look back!

The Lion dance is a traditional dance in several Asian cultures. During the dance, performers mimic a lion's movements while wearing a lion costume. The dance is done to bring good luck and fortune. The lion dance is usually performed during the Chinese New Year and other important occasions.

Coaching Note: Explain any words that your learner does not understand. You can't make an image if you don't know what to visualize!

PARAGRAPH TO QUESTIONS: PART 2

Visualize the previous text and answer these questions.

Describe your visualization of the Lion dance.

Why do people perform the Lion Dance?

Name one event where the Lion Dance is performed. How did you visualize that?

PARAGRAPH TO QUESTIONS: PART 1

Read the text below. Visualize the story as you read. Include as many details as you can in your brain movie.

Next, turn the page and answer the questions about the brain movie you created. Don't look back!

Chopsticks are eating utensils that were first used in the 3rd century. They can be made of metal or wood. When using wooden chopsticks, rub one chopstick against the other before you eat. This makes the chopsticks nice and smooth.

Coaching Note: Explain any words that your learner does not understand. You can't make an image if you don't know what to visualize!

PARAGRAPH TO QUESTIONS: PART 2

Visualize the previous text and answer these questions.

Describe the chopsticks you imagined.

What two materials can chopsticks be made of?

Demonstrate what you can do with wooden chopsticks before you eat.

PARAGRAPH TO QUESTIONS: PART 1

Read the text below. Visualize the story as you read. Include as many details as you can in your brain movie.

Next, turn the page and answer the questions about the brain movie you created. Don't look back!

Tokyo Sky Tree is a 634 meter tall tower in Tokyo, Japan. It is the tallest tower in the world. The Sky Tree has a great view of Tokyo and sometimes Mt Fuji is visible as well. There are lots of windows for viewing and even a see-through floor that you can stand on.

Coaching Note: Explain any words that your learner does not understand. You can't make an image if you don't know what to visualize!

PARAGRAPH TO QUESTIONS: PART 2

Visualize the previous text and answer these questions.

Describe how you imagine the Tokyo Sky Tree.

Name something that can be seen from the top.

Demonstrate what it would be like to stand on a see-through floor when you are that high. Did you include that in your movie?

----

2 PARAGRAPHS TO IMAGE: PART 1

Read the text below. Visualize the story as you read. Include as many details as you can.

Next, turn the page and draw an image from the movie you created in your brain. Include as many details as you can. Don't look back!

Basketball is very popular at my school. Many boys and girls play at recess and lunch. It is my favorite game, so most of the time I choose to play, too.

Some boys in my class do not like basketball. They think soccer is more fun. I like soccer, too, but basketball is number one for me.

Draw a picture from your brain movie.

Coaching Note: Use questions to elicit more details about your learner's image.

2 PARAGRAPHS TO IMAGE: PART 1

Read the text below. Visualize the story as you read. Include as many details as you can.

Next, turn the page and draw an image from the movie you created in your brain. Include as many details as you can. Don't look back!

Bullet trains are very fast, long distance trains in Japan. Amazingly, these trains travel at 320km/h. That's 200mph.

The trains have a green car (first class car) and an ordinary car (economy class car). Most bullet trains have reserved and non-reserved seat carriages. If you don't reserve during peak periods, you may not get a seat and you may end up standing for the trip.

Draw a picture from your brain movie.

Coaching Note: Use questions to elicit more details about your learner's image.

2 PARAGRAPHS TO IMAGE: PART 1

Read the text below. Visualize the story as you read. Include as many details as you can.

Next, turn the page and draw an image from the movie you created in your brain. Include as many details as you can. Don't look back!

LIONS PART 1

The lion is one of the five big cats in the genus *Panthera*. It is the second-largest cat after the tiger. Wild lions currently exist in Africa and in Asia. Until about 10,000 years ago, the lion was the most widespread large land mammal after humans.

Lions are unusually social compared to other cats. A pride of lions consists of related females and offspring and a small number of adult males. Groups of female lions typically hunt together.

Draw a picture from your brain movie.

Coaching Note: Use questions to elicit more details about your learner's image.

2 PARAGRAPHS TO IMAGE: PART 1

Read the text below. Visualize the story as you read. Include as many details as you can.

Next, turn the page and draw an image from the movie you created in your brain. Include as many details as you can. Don't look back!

LIONS PART 2

Lions are predators, but they are also expert scavengers. They can obtain over 50 percent of their food by scavenging. Lions are also nocturnal. This means that they are active primarily at night.

In the wild, males seldom live longer than 10 to 14 years. Injuries from fighting with rival males greatly reduce their lifespan. In captivity they can live more than 20 years.

Draw a picture from your brain movie.

Coaching Note: Use questions to elicit more details about your learner's image.

2 PARAGRAPHS TO TABLE: PART 1

Read the text below. Visualize the story as you read. Include as many details as you can in your brain movie.

Next, turn the page and list all the details you remember from your brain movie. Don't look back!

Dolly was a female sheep. She is famous because she was the first animal to be cloned. This means that she was not born from a mother and father. Instead, scientists "copied" her from the cells of another adult sheep.

Scientists took 277 attempts to create Dolly because cloning is very difficult. She was cloned at the Roslin Institute in Edinburgh, Scotland in 1996.

Coaching Note: Explain any words that your learner does not understand. You can't make an image if you don't know what to visualize!

2 PARAGRAPHS TO TABLE: PART 2

Note down all the details you can remember from your brain movie or from the story in the table below. No going back to check!

Some sections of the table may not have any details.

WHAT	
WHERE	
WHEN	
ACTION	
EMOTION	
RELATION	
SENSORY DETAILS (see, touch, taste, sound, smell)	

How many details did you visualize?_____

Write a one or two sentence summary of the story.

----

2 PARAGRAPHS TO TABLE: PART 1

Read the text below. Visualize the story as you read. Include as many details as you can in your brain movie.

Next, turn the page and list all the details you remember from your brain movie. Don't look back!

Laos is a country in Asia. It has a population of 7 million people. The capital is Vientiane.

There are many things to see if you go to Laos. There are Buddhist temples, wonderful food, and caves and waterfalls to see. You can go hiking and visit villages in the mountains.

Coaching Note: Explain any words that your learner does not understand. You can't make an image if you don't know what to visualize!

2 PARAGRAPHS TO TABLE: PART 2

Note down all the details you can remember from your brain movie or from the story in the table below. No going back to check!

Some sections of the table may not have any details.

WHAT	
WHERE	
WHEN	
ACTION	
EMOTION	
RELATION	
SENSORY DETAILS (see, touch, taste, sound, smell)	

How many details did you visualize?_____

Write a one or two sentence summary of the story.

----

2 PARAGRAPHS TO TABLE: PART 1

Read the text below. Visualize the story as you read. Include as many details as you can in your brain movie.

Next, turn the page and list all the details you remember from your brain movie. Don't look back!

The smallest fish in the world is called the dwarf pygmy goby or the Philippine goby. These gobies live in freshwater, seawater or brackish water environments. Brackish water is like a mix. It is a bit salty but not the same as sea water.

The dwarf pygmy goby is mainly a Philippine species. But, in 1992, a few were also found in Indonesia and Singapore. It was imported into Germany in 1958.

Coaching Note: Explain any words that your learner does not understand. You can't make an image if you don't know what to visualize!

2 PARAGRAPHS TO TABLE: PART 2

Note down all the details you can remember from your brain movie or from the story in the table below. No going back to check!

Some sections of the table may not have any details.

WHAT	
WHERE	
WHEN	
ACTION	
EMOTION	
RELATION	
SENSORY DETAILS (see, touch, taste, sound, smell)	

How many details did you visualize?_____

Write a one or two sentence summary of the story.

----

2 PARAGRAPHS TO TABLE: PART 1

Read the text below. Visualize the story as you read. Include as many details as you can in your brain movie.

Next, turn the page and list all the details you remember from your brain movie. Don't look back!

The most dangerous animal in the world is the box jellyfish. Box jellyfish live mostly in the ocean near Australia. They get their name from the cube-like shape of their bell.

Up to 15 tentacles grow from each corner of the bell and can be up to 10 feet long. Each tentacle has about 5,000 stinging cells. These stingers are not triggered by touch. They are triggered by chemicals on the skin of its prey.

Coaching Note: Explain any words that your learner does not understand. You can't make an image if you don't know what to visualize!

2 PARAGRAPHS TO TABLE: PART 2

Note down all the details you can remember from your brain movie or from the story in the table below. No going back to check!

Some sections of the table may not have any details.

WHAT	
WHERE	
WHEN	
ACTION	
EMOTION	
RELATION	
SENSORY DETAILS (see, touch, taste, sound, smell)	

How many details did you visualize?_____

Write a one or two sentence summary of the story.

----

2 PARAGRAPHS TO QUESTIONS: PART 1

Read the text below. Visualize the story as you read. Include as many details as you can in your brain movie.

Next, turn the page and answer the questions about the brain movie you created. Don't look back!

BURJ KHALIFA PART 1

The tallest building is called the Burj Khalifa. It is 2,722 feet tall, almost 1 kilometer!

Burj means tower in Arabic. Khalifa is the name of the leader of the United Arab Emirates.

Coaching Note: Explain any words that your learner does not understand. You can't make an image if you don't know what to visualize!

2 PARAGRAPHS TO QUESTIONS: PART 2

Visualize the previous text and answer these questions.

Describe the tower you imagined.

Khalifa is the name of a leader. Describe what you imagined for this word.

When you imagined the tower, where were you standing? Were you at the bottom, looking up? Or at the top, looking down?

----

2 PARAGRAPHS TO QUESTIONS: PART 1

Read the text below. Visualize the story as you read. Include as many details as you can in your brain movie.

Next, turn the page and answer the questions about the brain movie you created. Don't look back!

BURJ KHALIFA PART 2

The Burj Khalifa building is in Dubai. Most people think Dubai is a country. It is not. It is one of the seven Emirates in the United Arab Emirates.

Construction of the Burj Khalifa started in 2004 and finished in 2009. It was opened in 2010. It cost $1.5 billion to build.

Coaching Note: Explain any words that your learner does not understand. You can't make an image if you don't know what to visualize!

2 PARAGRAPHS TO QUESTIONS: PART 2

Visualize the previous text and answer these questions.

Where is the Burj Khalifa?

What did you imagine for Dubai?

It cost $1.5 billion to build. How did you imagine/visualize that?

----

2 PARAGRAPHS TO QUESTIONS: PART 1

Read the text below. Visualize the story as you read. Include as many details as you can in your brain movie.

Next, turn the page and answer the questions about the brain movie you created. Don't look back!

DONUTS

There are 3 types of donuts. Ring donuts are shaped like a ring. Filled donuts are round. They have jam, cream or chocolate inside.

There are also donut "holes". These are shaped like a small ball.

Coaching Note: Explain any words that your learner does not understand. You can't make an image if you don't know what to visualize!

2 PARAGRAPHS TO QUESTIONS: PART 2

Visualize the previous text and answer these questions.

What are the three types of donuts mentioned?

_____

_____

Describe the filled donut that you imagined. What was inside?

_____

_____

Describe how you imagined the donut hole. What flavour did you imagine?

_____

_____

2 PARAGRAPHS TO QUESTIONS: PART 1

Read the text below. Visualize the story as you read. Include as many details as you can in your brain movie.

Next, turn the page and answer the questions about the brain movie you created. Don't look back!

WHALE SHARK PART 1

The whale shark is the largest species of fish in the world. It may grow to more than twelve meters. Despite its size, the whale shark is normally a tame and harmless creature.

These sharks feed upon plankton, shrimp and small fish.

Coaching Note: Explain any words that your learner does not understand. You can't make an image if you don't know what to visualize!

2 PARAGRAPHS TO QUESTIONS: PART 2

Visualize the previous text and answer these questions.

What animal is this text about?

When you first started reading the text, did you imagine a dangerous creature? How did that change as you continued to read?

In you brain movie, how did the size of the shark's food compare to the size of the shark?

3+ PARAGRAPHS TO IMAGE: PART 1

Read the text below. Visualize the story as you read. Include as many details as you can.

Next, turn the page and draw an image from the movie you created in your brain. Include as many details as you can. Don't look back!

WHALE SHARK PART 2

The whale shark is a filter feeder, which means that it swims across the water with its mouth hanging open to catch food. The mouth has a powerful suction which draws in water and any food nearby.

Whales sharks are also migratory. This means they do not stay in the same place. They swim long distances.

They can be seen either on their own or in groups of up to several hundred sharks. Whale sharks reproduce by fertilizing eggs and releasing them into the water. This is how we get baby whale sharks.

Draw a picture from your brain movie.

Coaching Note: Use questions to elicit more details about your learner's image.

3+ PARAGRAPHS TO IMAGE: PART 1

Read the text below. Visualize the story as you read. Include as many details as you can.

Next, turn the page and draw an image from the movie you created in your brain. Include as many details as you can. Don't look back!

The richest country in the world is Qatar. One side of Qatar is next to Saudi Arabia. The rest of Qatar is surrounded by the waters of the Persian Gulf.

Qatar gets most of its money from oil. Before they found oil in Qatar, they made their money from fishing and hunting pearls.

Qatar is also very, very hot. The temperature goes above 50 degrees celsius!

Draw a picture from your brain movie.

Coaching Note: Use questions to elicit more details about your learner's image.

3+ PARAGRAPHS TO IMAGE: PART 1

Read the text below. Visualize the story as you read. Include as many details as you can.

Next, turn the page and draw an image from the movie you created in your brain. Include as many details as you can. Don't look back!

A desert is an area of land that is very dry. Not much rain falls in a desert. About one third of the land on Earth is a desert.

The largest hot desert is the Sahara. It is in northern Africa. It is nearly as large as the whole United States. The Sahara is hot during the day and cold at night.

The largest cold desert is Antarctica. Antarctica is the coldest place on Earth. When it snows, the snow does not melt. The snow builds up to make thick sheets of ice, called ice sheets.

Not many animals live in the desert. In hot deserts you can find lizards, snakes, and camels. Seals and penguins live in cold deserts.

Draw a picture from your brain movie.

Coaching Note: Use questions to elicit more details about your learner's image.

3+ PARAGRAPHS TO IMAGE: PART 1

Read the text below. Visualize the story as you read. Include as many details as you can.

Next, turn the page and draw an image from the movie you created in your brain. Include as many details as you can. Don't look back!

Paris is the capital of France. It is the largest city in France. More than 2 million people live in Paris.

Paris has many famous places, like the Eiffel Tower and the Louvre.

The Eiffel Tower is the most famous sight in Paris. It was built in 1889. More than 6 million people visit it every year.

The Louvre is a museum with many famous works of art. The Louvre is the third biggest museum in the world. More than 5 million people visit it each year.

I want to visit Paris one day!

Draw a picture from your brain movie.

Coaching Note: Use questions to elicit more details about your learner's image.

3+ PARAGRAPHS TO TABLE: PART 1

Read the text below. Visualize the story as you read. Include as many details as you can in your brain movie.

Next, turn the page and list all the details you remember from your brain movie. Don't look back!

An astronaut is a person who goes into space.

The first person in space was from Russia. His name was Yuri Gagarin. This happened on April 12, 1961.

The first person to walk on the moon was from America. His name was Neil Armstrong. He walked on the moon on July 20, 1969.

Some countries have worked together to build the International Space Station. Astronauts live on the space station for weeks or months. They do science experiments to learn more about living in space.

No one has visited any planets yet. Maybe you will do that when you grow up!

Coaching Note: Explain any words that your learner does not understand. You can't make an image if you don't know what to visualize!

3+ PARAGRAPHS TO TABLE: PART 2

Note down all the details you can remember from your brain movie or from the story in the table below. No going back to check!

Some sections of the table may not have any details.

WHAT	
WHERE	
WHEN	
ACTION	
EMOTION	
RELATION	
SENSORY DETAILS (see, touch, taste, sound, smell)	

How many details did you visualize?_____

Write a one or two sentence summary of the story.

3+ PARAGRAPHS TO TABLE: PART 1

Read the text below. Visualize the story as you read. Include as many details as you can in your brain movie.

Next, turn the page and list all the details you remember from your brain movie. Don't look back!

HOTEL STORY PART 1

My grandma is really cool. Last weekend, she took me and my little sister Tina to stay at a hotel.

I had never stayed at a hotel before. The first thing we did was check in. This is where you go to the big desk at the entrance. They give you your room key and tell you stuff about the hotel.

Our room was awesome. There was a bed for grandma. Tina and I got to sleep on the sofa bed. I have never slept on a sofa bed before.

After looking at the room, we all went down to the pool. Grandma stayed with Tina, but I was old enough to swim by myself. I even went to the deep end. I played with a boy about my age for a while.

Tina got tired. I was a bit tired too. So we went back to our room.

3+ PARAGRAPHS TO TABLE: PART 2

Note down all the details you can remember from your brain movie or from the story in the table below. No going back to check!

Some sections of the table may not have any details.

WHAT	
WHERE	
WHEN	
ACTION	
EMOTION	
RELATION	
SENSORY DETAILS (see, touch, taste, sound, smell)	

How many details did you visualize?_____

Write a one or two sentence summary of the story.

_____

_____

3+ PARAGRAPHS TO TABLE: PART 1

Read the text below. Visualize the story as you read. Include as many details as you can in your brain movie.

Next, turn the page and list all the details you remember from your brain movie. Don't look back!

HOTEL STORY PART 2

Do you remember what you read in part 1? I hope so. Here's the rest of the story.

The best part of the day came next. We got to order room service! This means that a waiter brings your food to your hotel room. I got to have dinner sitting on my bed!

My grandma said that this is a special treat. It sure is! My mom would never let me eat dinner in bed.

In the morning, we had muffins for breakfast. Then it was time to go home. This sure was a fantastic weekend.

3+ PARAGRAPHS TO TABLE: PART 2

Note down all the details you can remember from your brain movie or from the story in the table below. No going back to check!

Some sections of the table may not have any details.

WHAT	
WHERE	
WHEN	
ACTION	
EMOTION	
RELATION	
SENSORY DETAILS (see, touch, taste, sound, smell)	

How many details did you visualize?_____

Write a one or two sentence summary of the story.

Read the text below. Visualize the story as you read. Include as many details as you can in your brain movie.

Next, turn the page and list all the details you remember from your brain movie. Don't look back!

Hummingbirds are small colorful birds. They are found in North America and South America.

Hummingbirds are very interesting. They flap their wings really fast, about 80 times per second.

Hummingbirds can fly in all directions, even upside down! They can also hover in one place. They do this by flapping their wings in a pattern like an 8. They are the only bird that can do this.

Hummingbirds eat nectar, tree sap and pollen. They must eat often because they need lots of energy to flap their wings so fast. Their long beak helps them get nectar from flowers.

Coaching Note: Explain any words that your learner does not understand. You can't make an image if you don't know what to visualize!

3+ PARAGRAPHS TO TABLE: PART 2

Note down all the details you can remember from your brain movie or from the story in the table below. No going back to check!

Some sections of the table may not have any details.

WHAT	
WHERE	
WHEN	
ACTION	
EMOTION	
RELATION	
SENSORY DETAILS (see, touch, taste, sound, smell)	

How many details did you visualize?_____

Write a one or two sentence summary of the story.

_____

_____

3+ PARAGRAPH TO QUESTIONS: PART 1

Read the text below. Visualize the story as you read. Include as many details as you can in your brain movie.

Next, turn the page and answer the questions about the brain movie you created. Don't look back!

I want to go to Morocco! Morocco is a country in northern Africa. That is a long way from where I live.

I read a book about Morocco. It told me that there are many fun things to do. I want to walk through the markets and buy cool stuff. I also want to go see the Atlas mountains. It would be fun to hike somewhere so different.

Morocco is next to the Atlantic Ocean and the Mediterranean Sea. There are lots of beaches to visit. I would love to go swimming there as well.

There are two main languages in Morocco. They are Berber and Arabic. I do not know either. Maybe I should start learning!

Coaching Note: Explain any words that your learner does not understand. You can't make an image if you don't know what to visualize!

3+ PARAGRAPH TO QUESTIONS: PART 2

Visualize the previous text and answer these questions.

What did you visualize for Morocco's location?

What did you visualize for some of the activities that the author wants to do?

3+ PARAGRAPH TO QUESTIONS: PART 1

Read the text below. Visualize the story as you read. Include as many details as you can in your brain movie.

Next, turn the page and answer the questions about the brain movie you created. Don't look back!

THE LARGEST CRUISE SHIP

The Allure of the Seas is the world's largest cruise ship. It is 1187 feet long and 213 feet wide. It weighs more than 225,000 tons.

There are many things to do on the ship. There are swimming pools, gardens and a water show. The theater seats more than a thousand people. There is even an ice skating rink.

There are also many restaurants to choose from. As a passenger, you have 25 different choices of where to eat!

This ships sounds like a lot of fun. Do you want to come with me?

Coaching Note: Explain any words that your learner does not understand. You can't make an image if you don't know what to visualize!

3+ PARAGRAPH TO QUESTIONS: PART 2

Visualize the previous text and answer these questions.

What did you visualize for the appearance of the ship?

What did you visualize for the activities on the ship?

What did you visualize for the choice of restaurants on the ship?

3+ PARAGRAPH TO QUESTIONS: PART 1

Read the text below. Visualize the story as you read. Include as many details as you can in your brain movie.

Next, turn the page and answer the questions about the brain movie you created. Don't look back!

Basketball is a sport that was invented by James Naismith in 1891. That is more than one hundred years ago!

Basketball is played with an orange ball on a basketball court. A basketball court is a rectangle shape with hoops at each end. The hoop is a round circle that players must throw the ball through.

Basketball is very popular. It is the second most popular sport in the world. Basketball has been played in the Summer Olympic Games since 1936.

Coaching Note: Explain any words that your learner does not understand. You can't make an image if you don't know what to visualize!

3+ PARAGRAPH TO QUESTIONS: PART 2

Visualize the previous text and answer these questions.

Describe what you visualized for the time that basketball was invented.

Describe a basketball court.

What changed for basketball in 1936?

3+ PARAGRAPH TO QUESTIONS: PART 1

Read the text below. Visualize the story as you read. Include as many details as you can in your brain movie.

Next, turn the page and answer the questions about the brain movie you created. Don't look back!

Penguins are sea birds that live in Australia, New Zealand, South Africa and South America.

All penguins have a white belly and a dark back. Penguins have small wings, but they cannot fly. The wings help them swim, which is important for catching food.

Penguins eat krill, fish, squid and other small animals from the ocean.

Emperor penguins are the biggest type of penguin. They are about 4 feet tall. The smallest penguins, known as Little Penguins, are about one foot tall.

Coaching Note: Explain any words that your learner does not understand. You can't make an image if you don't know what to visualize!

3+ PARAGRAPH TO QUESTIONS: PART 2

Visualize the previous text and answer these questions.

Describe what you visualized for an emperor penguin.

Name three places where penguins are found.

How does a penguin's wings help it?

WHAT NEXT?

If this is your first time completing the workbook, your next step should be to complete the workbook again, this time doing it orally.

Check out the coaching instructions at the beginning of the book for more information on the oral approach.

By the time you have completed the oral version of the workbook, your learner will be able to describe the images they are making as they read 2-3 paragraph texts.

Your next step is to transfer this skill to reading real books.

Choose easy, visual stories and build up your learner's stamina at visualizing while they read. Start with questioning their mental image every few sentences and build up to a page or more at a time. Over time, increase the difficulty of books/texts until they are approaching or reach grade level.

As always, make it fun and reward good effort and progress.

Happy Reading!

If you found this book useful, please leave a short review on your favorite online bookstore. It makes an amazing difference for independent publishers like Happy Frog Press. Just two sentences will do!

Don't forget to look for other workbooks in the **Six-Minute Thinking Skills** series. The

Your learners might also benefit from our **Six-Minute Social Skills series**.

The workbooks in this series build core social skills for kids who have social skills challenges, such as those with Autism, Asperger's and ADHD.

Although numbered, these books can be used in any order.

CERTIFICATE
OF
ACHIEVEMENT

THIS CERTIFICATE IS AWARDED TO

_____

IN RECOGNITION OF

_____

_____   _____

DATE   SIGNATURE

101

Printed in Great Britain
by Amazon